LEGACY

3-Term Mayor

The Honorable Charles L. Albert Jr.

ISBN-13: 978-0-9996130-6-1

Library of Congress Control Number: 2021900067

Published 2021 by October Day Publishing L.L.C.

Printed in the United States of America

OCTOBER DAY
PUBLISHING

In Loving Memory of My Parents

Mr. Charles Albert Sr. and Mrs. Pearl Blue-Albert

***

This book is dedicated to my beautiful and supportive wife, Mrs. Ernie Tyson-Albert, the love of my life; our wonderful children: Reginald F. Albert, Cheryl Regina Albert, Rashad Albert; to our Grandchildren, Great Grandchildren, and Godchild.

***

To my Immediate and Extended Family Members, Friends
Pastor and Members of Prince Albert A.M.E. Church,
Civic and Political Acquaintances,
Elm Street Little League,
and all my Former Students

I cherish my relationship with each of you! It means a great deal that you've shared your life, love, and laughter with Ernie and me. I am sincerely appreciative of every kind gesture and every understanding heart.

May God richly bless all of you!

Table of Contents

Prologue

I'm Driven. Figuratively, my vehicle is controlled by a compelling desire to ensure the historical narrative of influential Black Americans who served their cities and small towns is forever preserved for generations. Anxious about this afternoon's interview is an understatement. Most of the questions I plan to ask are no longer rolling around in my head; they're on my laptop, a fact which encourages me to relax and focus on the drive.

Occupying the space where miles of green, thick forestry and undeveloped land once stood are new residential subdivisions, apartments, chain stores, medical facilities, and professional service buildings. Not many years ago, the view was mostly countryside the entire drive and nearly pitch black at night. Road construction and bright, eye-catching signage hoisted above strategically located buildings make the originally thirty-minute drive approximately one hour in heavy traffic.

The image of an intimidatingly huge logging truck trailer is coming into focus through my driver's side-view mirror. It's approaching quickly and presumably headed to one of the lumbermills on Amelia Island. The logs, likely tall pine trees, extend beyond the trailer's length, bound, and stacked horizontally on top of each other by something that appears to lack the strength of iron chains—but obviously can handle the load. The span of the cargo creates a menacing slow-motion illusion as it passes.

What's not an illusion is that the hard work and service-oriented contributions of Black Americans from small towns are often overlooked; their word-of-mouth accomplishments rarely make the national news. The City of Fernandina and its citizens work hard to be inclusive. Admittedly, they have not always adopted that perspective.

Downgraded tropical storm *Isaias* made the national news. It brushed the coast of Florida a few hours ago but quickly turned away. Between bouts of spontaneous sunshine, residual bands of heavy rainfall are playing games with my vehicle's rain-sensing automatic wipers. I can barely see the car ahead of me or the white line down the middle of the road through the front windshield—then suddenly, the rain stops, and I can see clearly. To my right, a low-hanging billboard along the two-lane stretch of State Road 200 A1A reads, "Drive-In Church Service, Sunday at 10 AM." It's creative, and weather permitting, many consider it a safe alternative to in-person worship service during this COVID-19 Pandemic.

I'll be recording this interview at his residence, located in a predominately Black neighborhood on South 11th Street. Encouraging me from the passenger's seat is my "Women Who Win" backpack containing my laptop, pens, paper, plus all my required personal protective equipment: latex gloves, mask, hand sanitizer, and a set of lapel microphones with six feet of extension. Nothing will sway my determination to carry out this in-person social distancing interview safely.

Ushering me across the Intracoastal Waterway and onto Amelia Island is the Thomas J. Shave Jr. Bridge and the sunshine that, again, just broke through the dreary grey clouds. As I approach the top of the bridge, large plumes of thick, white smoke from the Rayonier plant are visible across the Amelia River to the left. In a few miles, a small green highway sign to my right, near the sidewalk, reads, "Fernandina Beach City Limits."

Who is this man that so many on Amelia Island speak of highly? During his elected at-large tenure on the city commission, the town's positive socio-economic impact from 1978 through 1996 is indisputable. Yet, as of the year 2020, his name is not listed or acknowledged on any electronic or paper historical compilations of United States Black mayors.

Family, friends, and political acquaintances say the word "honorable" is an accurate representation of his personal character. Always striving for excellence with humility; he is *The Honorable Charles L. Albert Jr.*

Respectfully, this is his story.

The Oyster Cannery

In the wee hours of the morning, the Amelia River is dark and barely moving. A quarter-sized moon visible in the distant sky is quickly disappearing. The remainder of its low light glistens across the soft ripples of water quietly creeping close to the shore. In the dimly lit sky, patches of tall green and brown grassy marsh scattered within the brackish and muddy waters are intimidating to an unskilled fisher. It's the time just before dawn when oyster, shrimp, and crab fishermen begin their day.

***

The scenario:

In the 1930s, a group of skilled Black fishermen, living in the country, greet each other while reporting for work at the oyster cannery in Goffinsville. The one who routinely provokes comradery rallies the group.

"Les beat dat sun comin up and gather up dem oysters from da water. Y'all come on now, get yo gloves and grab dem hand tongs. Les push out on dat boat and dredge dis riva fo deez shells. Lawd, dis riva don't always smell nice, but dis is our life, dis is our money; and we get paid good."

A tardy co-worker is coming up on the rear of the group, fumbling to push a brown paper bag down in the big pocket on the side of his overalls. He shoulders through the crowd while big-mouth yawning, "Mornin Er'body!"

Somebody hollers, "Hey, look out now! What's dat I smell on yo breff? You know it is too early fo dat (the men roar with laughter). You been sippin dat shine again. If you tipsy dis early in da mornin, you gone lose your balance—en'up in dat cold riva wit sum crabs in yo britches!"

Waving off his co-workers getting their morning laugh, big-mouth yawning smirk's, "Aw man, whatchu talkin bout? You jes worry bout dem oysters and I worry bout makin sho dem crabs get in my net. Dats what you need to do!"

Another man wisecrack's, "Yeah, yeah, yeah! All he sayin is—it is too early fo dat. You know he right! Don't make us have to stop workin to save yo butt fum drownin!"

The last amused but contentious man, in a deep raspy voice, yells, "Dats truth, not lies! Summa da wives workin here— Dey waitin on a cert'n haul'a oyster to shuck, shrimp to head, and crab to cut. Dats extra money in our house cum payday. We out here fo'day in da mornin and you tipsy, messin wit our

[6]

money. I'm gone pour dat shine ova yo skull and sho nuff whip yo butt." Spontaneous hysterical laughter echoes in the twilight.

Several men throw a hand up in the air, a few of them shaking their caps, as they wave at the boss watching from a distance, as usual. "Mornin Mr. Goffin, we headed out to de water now. You got any new instructions fo us b'fo we leave?"

Mr. Goffin is familiar with the men's early morning shenanigans. He welcomes the light-heartedness and finds it entertaining. Mr. Goffin shakes his head left-to-right and yells, "No new instructions," and with his left index finger in the air, he rapidly points the men toward the boats.

***

In 1940, Mr. Saul S. Goffin, an immigrant of Russian descent and Jewish by faith, penned a letter to the local U.S. Postal Service requesting special addressing privileges and specific mail delivery instructions. According to preserved and archived documents, his correspondence was received and responded to by the U.S. Postal Service in Washington D.C., and the Department of Commerce - U.S. Coast and Geodetic Survey. Request granted. The plot of land Mr. Goffin fell in love with and purchased in the late 1800s was now the village officially named Goffinsville. This former settlement near the Amelia River, nestled within the unincorporated community of Nassauville, was home to an oyster cannery that changed hands a few times after the Civil War. Saul Goffin made numerous renovations, built a commissary, provided on-site homes for some of the canning plant employees, and set up a Village Post Office. He even coined his own money, for specific trading, in the form of tokens. This nearly self-supporting community (Goffinsville) provided decent jobs for many Black men and women living in and around Nassauville.

Many county roads were paved with the oyster shells transported from the processing plant in this 1930 picture.

Vintage image courtesy "Yesterday's Recollections II," by Jan Johannes Sr.

Charles L. Albert Jr.

I grew up near Goffinsville, and that area is very special to me. It brings back so many fond memories. Both of my parents worked for Mr. Goffin. My dad gathered oysters, and my mother headed shrimp, cut crabs, and shucked oysters. I was just a youngster at the time. In my mind, we were living good because we had a steady stream of income from both parents. My grandfather's name was Prince Albert, and he built our church in Goffinsville on land donated by Saul Goffin. He called it Prince Chapel. I am Godly proud that in the year 2020, our church is still thriving.

Talking with Mr. Goffin was enjoyable. Although he was Jewish, sometimes he would visit our church, sit in the congregation, and listen to the sermon. I just liked him. Mr. Goffin died in the 1950s. The oyster cannery changed hands several times, was eventually abandoned, and then the land was sold by his granddaughter to Nassau County. In July of 2009, the former site of Goffinsville was developed into a beautiful historic park with two fishing piers, a boat ramp, a children's playground, nature trails, a covered picnic area, and video surveillance—all dedicated to the memory of Mr. Saul S. Goffin. He was a kind-hearted businessman who gave my parents (and other Black Americans) hard to come by jobs.

Stepping-Stones

The Scenario:

An unpretentious walk home from school, thinking about how a young Black man from the country might become mayor one day, was interrupted by the cruelty of racial violence.

***

"Watch out, Charles!" his walking buddy yelled as he ducked and covered his head with both arms.

A broken, sharp-ended white brick thumps in front of Charles, slicing through the dirt and grass inches in front of his foot. Just in the nick of time, he simultaneously stops in his tracks and instinctively shoves his forearm upward to protect his face.

Infuriated, his friend cursed, raised two angry fists to the sky, and shouted into the wind, "Why they gotta throw bricks?"

Slowly lowering his arm below eye level allows Charles to see the tail end of a yellow school bus passing. It's full of White kids, a few of them hanging out the windows on one side, laughing, and shouting obscenities. Another piece of brick is hurled by a student leaning out a rear window of the moving bus. Fortunately, its impact is no longer a physical threat; the bus is too far away.

***

It became routine to watch out for flying pieces of bricks and rocks thrown by White kids after school. While he clearly remembered the trauma of those incidents, Charles refused to return hatred with hatred. He channeled anger and frustration into education. Charles found a productive way to use negative experiences as stepping-stones to build his character and integrity, strengthen his resolve, and ultimately catapult him into his dream career.

The Way It Was

On The Farm

Charles L. Albert Jr.

I was born June 29, 1932, and we lived down by Christopher Creek in Nassauville for a long time. My grandfather, Mr. Prince Albert, was disembarked on the border of Crane Island in the 1800s. He built our house before my dad married my mother. It was a big house on thirteen acres with separate rooms for my four brothers, two sisters, our parents, and our grandmother.

The design of our house was unusual. The kitchen and dining room were situated on a huge outside veranda. A large closed-in living room with a fireplace was on the backside of the kitchen, with a calming view of the river. Individual bedrooms for my parents, grandmother, and sisters were aligned down a long hallway, with separate doors, similar to the way rooms are aligned in a hotel or motel.

At the L-shaped bend approaching the end of the hallway were separate bedrooms for me and my brothers. We noticed it more on cold days, but it didn't seem to matter that each person exiting their bedrooms and entering the kitchen area had to face the weather on our huge open terrace. Eight of our thirteen acres was farmland with a horse, cows, chickens, and pigs. We planted crops, and when they grew, we developed them for food. Every morning, I woke up extra early to milk the cows, afterwards, I would get ready for school.

The Schoolhouse

Before 6th grade, Ms. Bessie Bryant taught the Black kids in a one-room wooden schoolhouse on Goffinsville Road. Ms. Bryant had no help; she was the principal, counselor, custodian, and everything else. We walked to school every day. Ms. Bryant said I was a high-level student because spelling, mathematics, and science were subjects that came easy to me. I focused on education to redirect most of the unprovoked racial hostility I regularly experienced during segregation.

When the teacher asked the class a question, I would answer first. If she selected another student, but they couldn't respond, I would give them the correct answer. I figured I was helping, but some of the guys got angry—they said I was acting like I knew too much.

When I got home from school, there was no television, and back then, we certainly didn't have video games. Now and then, I listened to "The Lone Ranger" show on the radio, but other than doing farm and house chores, I studied.

Chicken Coop

During the 6th grade, the one-room schoolhouses were consolidated by the State; and Black students were bussed to Peck High (Colored School #1) in Fernandina. The White kids had a different school and a new school bus that picked them up from various places near their homes. We weren't allowed to ride their bus due to segregation, and Peck High was nearly eight miles away.

Rev. L.F. Morrison, a local Black pastor from O'Neil, Florida, took it upon himself to make sure we made it to school. He purchased a small raggedy second-hand school bus. He fixed it up as best he could, picked up all the Black kids from the country in Goffinsvile and Nassauville, and then drove us to city school in Fernandina. A beat-up pale-yellow school bus full of Black kids from the country gazing out of the windows pulled up to Peck High school. Immediately, the city kids gave it a nickname. They would laugh and say, "Here come the chicken coop, here come the chicken coop!" After school, we jumped back on the bus with Rev. Morrison as the driver, and he dropped us off as close as possible near our homes in and around Nassauville. Walking home, it was always necessary to keep our distance when the school busses transporting the White kids were approaching and passing us along the road. For some cruel reason, a lot of them took pleasure in throwing bricks and rocks at us. I always made it home safely, but harboring hatred was not productive.

Approaching 7th grade, I took a part-time job. Every morning before school, barrels of crabs were waiting on me at a crab house in downtown Fernandina. I earned $20 per week, making sure seafood was steamed, boiled, and ready to be shucked and cleaned by the Black women hired for that job. It was a lot of work, but I enjoyed getting paid. My grades never suffered.

Night Fishing

When the sun started going down, my grandmother would remind dad and me to go out on the paddle boat to catch fish. We pushed the boat out at nightfall. My job was to row and keep it steady while he was casting the net. Most of the time, the mullet would be jumping. Together, we'd scale and clean the fish, and the next day, dinner would be hot fish and grits.

We had many great conversations out on that paddle boat. My dad told me, "No matter what, I want you to get an education. One day there may not be a need for this kind of labor. I want all my children to get an education and learn skills that will allow them to have more opportunities and get better jobs."

Seeing Green

Charlie is a name that was represented three times on our farm; me, my dad, and Charlie the horse. After school, it was often my duty to make sure Charlie, the horse, was fed, and we knew he would only eat smooth cordgrass. Sometimes the marsh we collected would quickly turn brown. Charlie, the horse, refused to eat brown grass; it had to be green.

My brother, Prince, came up with an idea. Whenever the grass we collected from along the creek turned colors, he would place a green transparent shield over the horse's eyes. It's funny. Charlie ate every blade of that brown grass because what he saw temporarily looked green.

Hungry Bullies

The first time they took my bag lunch, the word must have gotten around Peck High School in the city that my mother makes the best fried fish and cornbread with that good crust on the ends. Sometimes, I was ashamed of my lunch when I should have been grateful. Our family had unrestricted use of Christopher Creek for fishing, plus a good income from employment. Many of my schoolmates were not as fortunate.

The guys at school would rouse me and say, "Hey man, what you hiding in that bag? Where's that lunch, where's that lunch?"

I would either have cold fish and grits or cold fish and cornbread hidden in my overalls, but the guys wanted my food. They kept at me almost every day.

"Hey Charles, whatever food you got in that bag, we want it, hand it over!"

There was no excuse for their behavior—but they probably needed it more than me. For that reason, I didn't mind being hungry some days.

God Told Me

Pretty Valedictorian

Charles L. Albert Jr.

Her name was Ernie Tyson back then; I met her for the first time in 6th grade after our one-room schoolhouse was consolidated and we were bussed to city school. She grew up to be the pretty valedictorian, Peck High Class of 1949, and I believe God told me she was gonna be my wife.

After I arrived home from school, I sat up until late in the evenings talking with my siblings about all those pretty girls at city school. My mother overheard us one day, and she said, "Look here, boy, let me tell you one thing! I ain't sending you to that school to look at no pretty girls. I am sending you there to get an education, and you better get an education!"

I watched Ernie from a distance for a while. When some of the other girls were clowning and sipping moonshine from a milk bottle, Ernie was in Home Economics Class sewing; other times, she'd be reading, writing, and making good grades. She and I knew we were not supposed to be sipping that shine. Ernie said the teachers never found out, but I say those teachers knew that bottle was being passed around in class. That moonshine odor permeated the whole room. I remember one teacher would sit at her desk and read her papers, pretending like nothing was going on—but she knew, they all knew.

Turning Collars

Ernie Tyson-Albert

The guys and the girls had to take Home Economics for a grade at Peck High. Our teacher, Mrs. Kennedy, assigned the entire class the same project. We were instructed to turn a collar on a man's shirt—change it, if it was worn or turn it around, if it was in good condition. I got so tickled; Charles couldn't do it. Every time he brought his project for the teacher to inspect, she would start fussing and berate him in front of the entire class.

Ms. Kennedy shouted, "Take that thing back to the house, you know better than that! Next time you better bring it back right. Go back to your seat!"

Charles was smart, but Home Economics was not his thing. He got fussed at so many times. Finally, he turned away from the teacher's desk and slowly walked back to his seat. He was so dejected and looking two shades darker than a crow! Before he passed my seat, I gritted my teeth and whispered, "Gimme that shirt!" and snatched it out of his hands. I shoved my completed project in his chest, and he sat down, quietly pretending to fix the mess he made. In no time, I turned the collar on the shirt he botched then gave it back to him. He presented it to Ms. Kennedy, as if he'd done the work. She praised him out loud.

"I knew you could do it; you took a long time, but you did it!"

Charles proudly walked back to his seat with his chest stuck out, looked at me, and smiled. He leaned towards my ear and confidently whispered, "The Lord told me you gonna be my wife." I laughed and told him, "Get-on away from here!"

***

Charles L. Albert Jr.
Yes. Home Economics was perilous times for me! That teacher was not gonna give me a good grade if I didn't correctly turn that collar. I tried for two weeks, but Ernie turned that collar in ten minutes!

Ernie Tyson-Albert
To this day, Charles still proclaims that God spoke to him about me. He grins, tilts his head backwards, puts both hands in the air and dramatizes how he looked up into the sky and heard God's voice say, "She gonna be your wife!"

The Prom

The Fernandina Beach Peck High, Class of 1949, was preparing for graduation. Before the commencement ceremonies comes the usual senior prom. But, choosing a date for this prom would be anything but traditional for Charles L. Albert Jr.

The Scenario:

Her voice echoed down the hallway on the school's second floor in a determined yet respectful tone. "Charles, let me ask you a question."

It's not as if she had a pool of guys to choose from; he was one of only three young men left in their graduating class of nine. Most of the guys dropped out of school in eighth grade to work at the Rayonier plant.

She's the apple of his eye. He can easily identify her voice above the chatter of students in the hallway, even when his back is turned. Charles stops in his tracks and calmly walks back toward her.

"Sure, Ernie, what's your question?" The pretty class valedictorian has his undivided attention.

"How would you like to be my date to the prom?" Ernie Tyson knew Charles was sweet on her, so she was almost certain he would say yes.

Charles wonders whether Ernie would have turned him down had he asked her to be his date first. He quickly redirects his thoughts and answers her question with a question. "Are you sure your parents won't mind me escorting you?"

Ernie assures him, "They're okay with it. They would prefer that a boy from my graduating class take me anyway."

Charles agrees and immediately begins planning. But days later, in the men's restroom, he eavesdrops on some guys talking. "Man, those corsages them girls pin on their dresses cost money. We ain't spending no extra money on a flower that ain't even gonna live long enough to get the value out of it!"

In St. Mary's, Georgia, Ernie's large family can't wait to travel to Fernandina Beach to witness the commencement ceremonies, meet her date, and see the beautiful prom dress her dad purchased. They all loaded into the pickup truck, including grandma's favorite rocking chair, and arrived the day of the prom.

Ernie's house was directly across the street, adjacent to the school. Charles arrived at her door on time in a nice suit to escort her to the prom. He didn't know her family from Georgia was in the house waiting to meet him.

Ernie opens the door in her beautiful dress, greets Charles then suddenly notices the prom date protocol is off. She bluntly blurts out, "Where's my flower?"

The tone of Ernie's voice alerts her grandma, who makes her way towards the front door in Ernie's defense. "Oh no he didn't!" grandma shouts. "My granddaughter is not a two-bit tramp. How dare you show up without a flower for her?"

The more grandma argues, the more Charles begins slowly backing out of the house. Why did he listen to those guys in the restroom? While grandma is stirring up the other family members, Charles tries to explain what happened, but no one is listening; Ernie needs a corsage!

Charles tunes out the family's frantic brainstorming chatter and starts to reminisce.

"...My mother took an extra job doing laundry. She gave me the money for Ernie's corsage in advance. I remember her pulling it out of her brassiere and happily shoving it into my hands."

Charles incorrectly assumed the opinion of the guys in the restroom represented the consensus. He learned a lesson about trying to fit in with the crowd.

He concluded, "From now on, I'll be making my own decisions!"

Charles' focus turns back to the family discussion about the corsage. He notices that Ernie's quick-thinking creative aunt had come up with an alternative and was putting it together. Since the floral shop was closed, Ernie's aunt went outside the house and picked several fresh flowers from the yard. Rumor has it that Ernie wore the most beautiful fashioned corsage at the prom. A prom date fiasco was averted for Charles, and as always, Ernie was graciously forgiving.

For Love

Ernie Tyson-Albert

My girlfriends convinced me to hang out with them in downtown Fernandina. I was supposed to go home after school, but I followed the crowd. We stopped in this photography studio and had our pictures taken. The other girls went back and paid for their photos. But there was no way on earth I was going to tell my parents I was downtown sitting in front of a camera, and then ask for their hard-earned money to pay for my disobedience. Somebody told me my picture was sitting in the window for everybody to see. I was nervous and scared my parents would find out what I did. I couldn't sleep at night thinking one day they would pass by the studio and see it displayed, but it wasn't even there anymore. Little did I know; Charles had purchased it and carried it with him overseas.

Charles L. Albert Jr.

When I finally came back from Japan, Ernie and I talked a lot. I explained to her why I purchased her picture from the photography studio. We began dating, but she still felt I wasn't serious about her. One day on the beach, we discussed my hesitation with going back to college. I felt I would be out-of-place among all those young high school graduates, or simply too old.

Ernie yelled at me. "What! Well, I'm telling you right now; there's nothing wrong with farmers, but I don't want to marry one. If you don't go to college, you better forget about me!"

What she said knocked me to my knees. Literally, the next day I was enrolling in college. I gave my application to the postman and entered Florida A&M University's Bachelor of Science Degree program in Tallahassee, Florida. Ernie graduated from college in 1955. Love prevailed, and I proposed to her under the moonlight while walking along American Beach. Ernie and I became husband and wife on June 7, 1958.

One day, I was thinking and feeling gratitude about the number of youth and young men I've had a chance to mentor. I proclaimed to my wife, "All I desire is a station wagon full of boys."

She laughed sarcastically and replied, "What! From who?"

Forensics in Japan

During the Korean Conflict (June 1950 - July 1953), the U.S. Army depended on scientific tests performed by troops specially trained to locate, recover, inter (or disinter), and perform autopsies on the remains of fallen American soldiers. Charles Albert was drafted nearing his second year at Edward Waters College, Jacksonville, Florida. When he began his tour of duty at Fort Benning, South Carolina, the military quickly recognized his love for science. Charles Albert was assigned the Military Occupational Specialty (MOS) Code: Graves Registration Service Group (1953-1955).

The Scenario:

One pair of ivory white dice click, clatter, and glow in the moonlight like oddly shaped chunks of bones on a black velvet backdrop as they roll across the weather deck of an Army sea vessel. If an unoccupied corner proved to be appropriate, several Graves Registration troops could be seen huddled in groups of two or more shooting craps for hours, winning and losing money. The game was a welcomed distraction to keep the men from thinking about why they were on a ship headed for the rice paddies and jungles of Korea in the middle of a war, not to fight, but to do a gruesome yet essential task that nobody wanted to perform.

***

"Alright, soldier, ante up! Slap the cash down right here if you wanna play." Dewayne unfolds a ten-dollar bill and says, "Now, put yours down."

Walter reaches into his pocket for cash. He squats next to Dewayne. "Ok, let's do it. I match your ten; the high roller is the shooter. Go ahead, throw 'em!"

Dewayne rolls a ten, Walter rolls a five. Dewayne shoots first. He shakes the dice in his loosely closed right fist, and then blows on them for luck. He tosses them across the deck and they bounce off the wall. "Humph, Dewayne mutters; five and four." He must repeat that shot to keep control of the dice.

Walter taunts him, laughing out loud. "Bet you won't roll that nine again. Shoot!

Dewayne rolls again, but it's a seven. Walter wins the pot and the dice.

The adrenaline from this quick win is spontaneously addictive to Walter; he happily blurts out, "That's my money, soldier. Now let's bump this game up. I got twenty. Match me!"

***

Charles L. Albert Jr.

The Army tested me and determined I was interested in science, microscopes, and chemistry. After Boot Camp, I was given specific training in preparation for my MOS assignment. Shortly after that, I shipped out for Korea on the William O. Darby.

More than 30,000 U.S. troops died during wartime. I was one of the troops tasked with combing Korea's jungles to retrieve the remains of American soldiers. I understood the importance of my job, yet I dreaded going into that jungle. I imagined the heat and the smell of decomposing corpses, trapped under wrecked equipment or vessels, some floating in-and-out with the tide, and blood all over my clothes. I needed to get control of my thoughts.

I prayed in my bunk on the ship every night for about two weeks. Some of my comrades were rolling dice; maybe that was their way of dealing with the same nightmarish dread I was experiencing. But I was having a conversation with God, asking him to turn that situation around for us.

One thing that kept my morale up and gave me hope was Ernie's picture inside my locker. I returned home on a 30-day furlough before going overseas to Korea. While walking around downtown Fernandina Beach, I saw this picture in the window of the photography studio. It was the only Black girl's picture looking at me through the large paned glass, and I knew who she was. I went inside the studio and asked the owner if he would sell it to me. According to the photographer, her picture had been there for more than a month and was never retrieved.

I paid him for the photo and took it with me overseas. When my locker door was open, the soldiers would walk by and ask me, "Who that pretty girl, man?" I enjoyed boasting and telling them she was my future wife, the apple of my eye. I still believed it was all part of God's plan.

***

At 5:00 AM one morning, the helmsman's voice blared through the ship's intercom, "Guys, I want y'all to know that we are NOT going to Korea; the war is over!"

I jumped out of my bunk and reiterated, "Y'all can put them dice away. We are not going to Korea!"

We debarked in Yokohama, Japan, and spent the remainder of our tour at a location called Camp Kokura. I worked in a laboratory and was responsible for opening body bags and caskets to identify the remains of fallen soldiers that had been located, shipped to the camp, and unloaded with dignity.

The detailed process of proper identification was critical to the Army. We examined any remains, including fingerprints, teeth, hair color, skin color, tattoos, scars, shoe size, dentures, bones, and personal effects.

No embalming was performed until there was no more doubt about the service members' identity—and we received the all-clear to send their remains home for a respectful military burial. It was indeed something that nobody wanted to do, but a necessary occupation, and I took pride in my assignment.

The Train Ride

Charles L. Albert Jr.

I am a huge Dodgers Baseball fan. When I think back on my childhood, I wish there had been an opportunity for me to participate in youth sports. I traveled a lot and often got the chance to watch kids between the ages of 9- and 12-years old play Little League baseball games. My hometown was a different story. There was no organized activity program for Black males to give them a sense of pride, build their self-esteem, and keep them busy after school. The only Little League team in Fernandina during the 60s was deemed "Whites Only."

My wife and I traveled to Portland, Oregon, for our honeymoon. During the train ride, I saw a group of young people (Blacks and Whites) playing on the same baseball team! We visited my aunt, whose little boy also played ball with the Little League. The entire trip home on the train, I thought about ways to get around that stumbling block called segregation and create the same opportunities for Black kids in my community. In 1966, the "Whites Only" Little League organization said Black kids wouldn't be able to understand the game and would have trouble fitting in with the segregated team. I was confident Black youth were intelligent and able to succeed in the sport if trained. I presented my ideas to some friends: Esdene Handsome, Archie B. Coakley, and Curtis Telfair Sr. They worked diligently to create a chartered organization. The teams were not yet integrated, so I trained and coached the Black males in a separate field on Elm Street. My oldest son was too young to play, so he first served as bat boy.

The community was amazed at how fast the youth learned the rules of the game and their highly competitive skill level. Several influencers used their voice on our behalf and explained to the segregated Little League organization that our guys were trained and ready.

It was my pleasure to be acknowledged as Elm Street Little League's official founder and serve as the Black league's first president and coach. Thankfully, the league has long since integrated. The youth have proudly been winning awards and championships. These results are always good news. Playing sports and participating in extra-curricular activities gives kids a huge confidence boost, and it matters to me that they can do it together.

***

In 1993, a lighted softball/baseball field with covered dugouts and bleachers; a concession stand; restrooms; three pavilions; a batting tunnel; an adjacent covered playground; as well as the Martin Luther King Jr. softball and baseball practice field, was named honorably by the City of Fernandina Beach, Florida: "Charles L. Albert Jr. Field."

Educators

Eighth Grade Science Teacher

PHOTO COURTESY OF CHARLES & ERNIE ALBERT

His childhood dream was to become mayor, but truth be told, teaching is what he loved more. It's one of the most underpaid and under-respected professions, yet greatly needed. After attaining his B.S. Degree in Biology from FAMU, Mr. Albert received a nine-month opportunity to positively impact lives at the Marianna School for Delinquent Boys in Florida. He studied Organic Chemistry at Tuskegee Institute; Chemical Bond Approach Chemistry at College of Saint Teresa; and Biological Science at Wake Forest University. He studied at Institute of Marine Science, Edward Waters College of Jacksonville, and University of North Florida. He was awarded "Teacher of the Year" in 1985 and served on the Nassau County School Board for two years.

Mr. Albert, the educator, was quick-witted, a fun teacher, observant of his students, but didn't take any mess from them. He recalled several young people who tried to pull the wool over his eyes, but he would always prove they could not outsmart him. On any given day, his science classroom would become a laboratory, and his students might recount the following scenario:

***

Mr. Albert walks into the classroom, pushing a cart with a bunch of different supplies: goggles, gloves, a deep bucket, and some other items sealed in small containers. The chatter of curious students fills the room.

"What is Mr. Albert carrying?"

"What is he going to do with those big plastic glasses?"

Mr. Albert has provoked their curiosity as he often does. The class is distracted, chattering, and can barely hear their names during roll call.

"Alright. Cut the frivolity! Today, we're going to do an experiment while we learn."

Mr. Albert fills the bucket with water and sets it upon a table that stands slightly higher than his student's desks. He puts the safety goggles over his eyeglasses. His students must stand near their seats or in small groups for the safest view of whatever might happen. Everyone watches as he opens one of the smaller containers and pinches off less than a pea-sized amount of something. Then, with a long tool for distance, he drops the substance into the water. His students are shocked and surprised to see sparks fly from the water's surface in the bucket. Mr. Albert elaborates, then opens the other small container and repeats the process. This time, a tiny fire, then suddenly a muffled explosion forcefully splashes water out of the bucket onto the table and floor. There's a shriek from the girls, and the boys shout, "Whoa, that was great!"

Mr. Albert smiles, removes his protective eyewear and gloves, then heads to the chalkboard. His back is turned to the class as he writes and explains the scientific symbols out loud.

"(Na) Sodium; (K) Potassium; (H20) Water; (H) Hydrogen Gas…".

Science class has begun.

Ernie Tyson-Albert Library

A good man generally has a good woman standing alongside him. Charles and Ernie Albert are educators, highly respected pillars of the community—both worthy of honor.

Charles Albert knew Ernie was extraordinary the minute he laid eyes on her in sixth grade. Although he didn't get a chance to hold a meaningful conversation with her until much later, he watched the way she carried herself from afar. When they married, she was his biggest supporter during his campaigning and his tenure. Mr. Albert speaks lovingly of how Ernie always understood and never complained when his civic duties called for long hours. He smiles when she talks and laughs at her recollections of amusing situations in which he sometimes found himself.

The woman that stands alongside the Honorable Charles L. Albert Jr. is a graduate of Florida A&M University, an Early Childhood Learning educator, and an advocate for the Black community. Like her husband, she has always been committed to excellence and passionate about the learning abilities of 3-to7-year-olds. Her constant concern could be the reason for the dream she had, which led her to the conclusion that "...the

Black kids in this community are not retarded; they simply haven't been taught how to read."

After retiring from the education system, and while Peck High was under renovation, Marie Stevenson (her friend over the After School Program) encouraged Mrs. Albert to inquire about using an empty classroom to teach kids how to read. Until they procured books for the children, Ernie collected and used old newspapers to drill reading and comprehension skills. Her creativity and determination quickly paid off. Before long, the children were reading and interpreting paragraphs.

IMAGE COURTESY OF FERNANDINA BEACH CITY COMMISSION WEBSITE

Mrs. Albert and her volunteers began networking with organizations that freely donated boxes of old books and library equipment. Some of the reading materials were in poor condition. It took lots of time and effort to clean them up. Eventually, the room in which Mrs. Albert initially taught fourth grade morphed into an official library.

In June of 2019, the Fernandina Beach City Commission unanimously agreed to name the library in her honor. To date, it contains more than 5,000 new adult and children's books and is operated solely by volunteers.

Throwback Thursday

In March of 2018, The City of Fernandina Beach Government graciously honored Mr. Albert "the educator" from its website. Many of the students he taught in Science, Math, Chemistry, and Biology chimed in on the City's "Throwback Thursday" Facebook post with heartfelt and lighthearted memories.

***

Ernie Tyson-Albert

They printed out a bunch of pages and handed them to me. When I started reading all those comments the students made on Facebook, Mr. Albert and I were smiling. We read all of them; a few were so funny! Mr. Albert remembered all his former students when I said each of their names. He would say, "Yeah, I remember," then he would get so tickled. Please share these. I want everyone to know Charles cared for his students, and he wanted each of them to be successful in life, whatever career they chose. I believe they love him because he was genuine and down to earth.

Paula Staten- Morris
Great man! 3

Like · Reply · 2y

Tracy Dunman-Weaver
Mr Albert was a huge part of my little world as a kid. I think of him often . Long after my school days i had the honor of caring for his mother in her final days . I wept with the family as she passed from this world into eternity. He became more than my old teacher, mayor, role model and mentor that day. I hugged him and we were family at that moment. He impacted me in so many ways . He resides in a little corner in my heart forever. Mr. Albert if you read this i hope you have a small understanding of how special you are and what you have meant to this community and the scores of children you have blessed. You are a giant, sir. You have brightened this corner of the world and this world is a better place because you are in it. Love always..

Like · Reply · 38w

Mark Thomas
Was ten minutes behind the bell cause we were in the woods behind his classroom burning with Mary Jane walked into to class with no excuse pass as to why I was late my statement to him was the ol got stuck in the restroom and he said Thomas no you weren't you have got things stuck on your pants that tell me you have been stuck in the woods now go sit down before I stick you in detention Thomas

Like · Reply · 38w ☺ 1

James D Weaver
U probably don't remember me. I drove u crazy in middle School. But, you were one of the best teachers I ever had. Thank you.

Like · Reply · 36w

Faye Carter
Made this young girl love science and enjoy doing so! Thanking God that our life's paths crossed!

Like · Reply · 2y 3

Stephen Finch
Charles Albert was a dedicated teacher and helped many students in school and in the community.

Like · Reply · 2y 3

> **Stephen Finch**
> And he still works to help people.
>
> Like · Reply · 1y

[44]

Donald Bagley

Had Mr. Albert as a teacher. Is funny,down to earth, tell you how it is. But still a great role model.

Like · Reply · 2y　　　　　　　　　　　　　　　　　　　　　　　　　　　　2

Natalie Van Wagner

Awe what a great man - thanks for making 8th grade biology memorable - luv & hugs Nat "Burger King" McRae

Like · Reply · 2y　　　　　　　　　　　　　　　　　　　　　　　　　　　　3

Jeff Proctor

A true role model for many generations, nothing but fond memories of Mr. Albert!!

Like · Reply · 2y　　　　　　　　　　　　　　　　　　　　　　　　　　　　4

Stevie Allen

Everyone has that one teacher who they will always remember abd for me, it's Mr. Albert. (it's time for court!)

Like · Reply · 1y　　　　　　　　　　　　　　　　　　　　　　　　　　　　5

Kim Parker Grubbs Aifd

Very classy man. I met him while he taught my daughters. He has made such a great impact in this town.

Like · Reply · 2y　　　　　　　　　　　　　　　　　　　　　　　　　　　　2

Kevin Leary

Great man , great mentor , great teacher. Can't believe no one has mentioned his movie career (The Sunshine state). Will have to take him some MORE fish now that I hear it's his fave.

Like · Reply · 2y　　　　　　　　　　　　　　　　　　　　　　　　　　　　11

Jessica Bruland

What an awesome teacher, member of our community and human!

Like · Reply · 2y　　　　　　　　　　　　　　　　　　　　　　　　　　　　3

Mark Davis

mr albert comes from a deep rooted Nassau county family , one of the best teachers we had in school as well as a devoted community leader , lets not forget all his family is top notch as well

Like · Reply · 2y　　　　　　　　　　　　　　　　　　　　　　　　　　　　8

Johnny Crawford

Cherished and respected friend, gentleman, servant-leader!

Like · Reply · 2y　　　　　　　　　　　　　　　　　　　　　　　　　　　　3

Joyce Mason

AMEN YES HE IS ONE OF THE. BEST THEACHERS FBH EVER HAD😂😂

Like · Reply · 2y　　　　　　　　　　　　　　　　　　　　　　　　　　　　1

[45]

Robbie Braddock
Mr. Albert was one of my favorite teachers. Class act gentleman.

Like · Reply · 2y 3

Lynann Mullis
One of my favorite teachers! 2 years of Science in Jr. High.

Like · Reply · 2y 1

Pamela Moore Phillips
Mr. Albert, you can never ever feel unloved! You truly have an amazing legacy, especially as a teacher! Thank You!

Like · Reply · 2y 3

Brenda Williams
He is such a wonderful man with high standards and a great role model for all! Everyone loves and respects him!

Like · Reply · 2y 8

Judy Lee
Definitely a wonderful man that has been a mentor and friend!!

Like · Reply · 2y 2

Michael E. Taylor Jr.
Mr. Albert is one of best and a true pillar on the island and in the county!

Like · Reply · 2y 5

Debra McDonald
Mr. & Mrs. Albert are BOTH amazing folks😍

Like · Reply · 2y 4

Trey Palmer
He was such a great teacher!

Like · Reply · 2y 3

Laurie Michelle
One of my first teachers when we moved to Fernandina. Loved him to pieces!

Like · Reply · 2y 3

Sonja Davis
He was the best teacher!! I loved his class!

Like · Reply · 1y

Betty Bell
Ask Mr Albert to tell u about the first time Earnie cooked oysters for his dinner!! Better than that his fishing boat that had "a little bit of water in the bottom ".

Like · Reply · 2y 2

Willie Scott
GIVE THEM THEIR FLOWERS. JOB WELL DONE

Like · Reply · 1y   1

Teresa Reynolds
I loved Mr. Albert as a teacher. In 8th grade, we put a whoopi cushion in his chair
and he smiled then immediately became stern. Still makes me laugh today thinking
of it. Such a great sense of humor and dedicated educator. He is at the top of my list
of favorites!

Like · Reply · 2y   14

🏆 Top Fan
Elaine Smith Coats
Honored and blessed to know him.

Like · Reply · 1y   2

Tonya Bennett Thornton
Amazing man! His wife, Ernie Albert was my first grade teacher and by far one of the
best ever!! Love this family!! 🖤 🖤

Like · Reply · 2y   2

Beth Boles
Mr. Albert was an amazing Jr. High science teacher - one of my favorites! Always a
kind, thoughtful gentleman with a quick wit. Did you know his middle name is
Laverne? 😊

Like · Reply · 2y   5

↳ 1 Reply

Miriam Traeye
🖤 my Rattler Alumni friend! 🐍 Fangs Up!! Awesome man!

Like · Reply · 2y   2

Ann Christensen McGrath
More kind than can be put into words. He was an amazing teacher!

Like · Reply · 2y   2

Shannon Smith
Love Mr Albert. So many accomplishments to be proud of. He was my teacher.

Like · Reply · 1y   1

Vanessa Lang
Mr.Albert is such a lovely men, beautiful soul beautiful heart ,awesome teacher, love
his people and what do anything he can for you I love him with all my heart
blessings to you and hope you have a wonderful marvelous rest of your life 😊 😊 🙏
🙏

Like · Reply · 1y · Edited

[47]

Lisa Mac Donald
Mr. Albert was definitely one of the good ones.

Like · Reply · 1y   ⊙ 1

Kelly Van Wagner Mcgregor
Definitely one of my favorite teachers of all time couldn't help but laugh at him when he would get on to me which was often but he never failed to keep pushing me love him.

Like · Reply · 1y   ⊙ 1

Thomas A Sanders
Definitely a Pioneer of the Community - KUDO!!!!!!!

Like · Reply · 2y   ⊙ 2

Terrell Stewart Sr
He gave me and **Rashad Gogators Al** the Nick name's flash and to quick when we was playing football together what a wonderful man I used to go stay many of nights where they accepted me with open arms the best road model in the world.

Like · Reply · 2y   ⊙ 4

Eric Higginbotham
Love me some Charles Albert

Like · Reply · 2y   ⊙ 4

Synetta Lawson
I love Mr. Albert! He is the best! A great role model for so many. Nonjudgemental, caring, and always has a smile.

Like · Reply · 2y · Edited   ⊙❤ 9

Jennifer Murray
Proud to say this is my great uncle!!

Like · Reply · 2y   ⊙ 1

Dana B. Strickland
One of my most favorite teachers! ☺ ♥

Like · Reply · 2y   ⊙ 2

> **Terri Long**
> Mine too! ⊙ 1
>
> Like · Reply · 2y
>
> **Maggie Adams**
> Mine too!   ⊙ 1
>
> Like · Reply · 2y

[48]

Alex Croft

I had him as a substitute teacher in school. He's an amazing man. Someone like that, you just never forget!

Like · Reply · 2y   3

Teri Pipkin Bradley

Mr Albert one of my favorite teachers. He is a great man!

Like · Reply · 1y   1

Valencia Dubberly Gower

Mr. Albert was a fabulous teacher and all round wonderful human being. Had him for 7th and 8th grade science. Learned all the bones and muscles. Hoping life is treating him well.

Like · Reply · 2y   6

> **Beth Boles**
>
> Yesss!! I remember having to stand in front of the class and name all the bones in the skeleton and all of the muscles on the diagram! He certainly made science fascinating. 😊
>
> Like · Reply · 2y

> **Pauline Love McKendree**
>
> Don't forget the periodic table.
>
> Like · Reply · 1y   1

Cassandra Floyd

So cool!   1

Like · Reply · 2y

Carla Creamer Higginbotham

Mr Albert you have always been such a gentleman and a great teacher! My first thought of you is you always saying "Creamer when you get through talking we will start class....

Much respect and appreciation for all you have done for all of us

Like · Reply · 2y   10

Quentin Gilbert

The G.O.A.T, Mr. Albert, definitely a icon here in our community

Like · Reply · 2y   3

Paula McGowen

Mr.Albert was and is a Blessing to me

Like · Reply · 2y   1

[49]

Ginger Hair
It was such an honor to have him for my science teacher. Learned a lot about science but also learned so much more. Kindness, Respect Manners and just good ole fashion learning. No fooling around or game playing. He was there to teach and the lesson he taught was there for the taking because he always gave it his all. Thank you Mr. Albert for a job well done 👍

Like · Reply · 1y   👍 2

Angeline Rainey Crawford
And he was a great and respected teacher!

Like · Reply · 2y   👍 2

Sandy Zachary
LOVE this sweet man!! 💕

Like · Reply · 2y   👍 2

Laura Dotson McMullan
Love this man!

Like · Reply · 2y   👍 2

Miriam Bailey Hannigan
What a wonderful man and educator! Thank you for your many years of dedication!

Like · Reply · 2y   👍 2

Kent Jones
Wow. What an appropriate tribute. My best to you, Mr. Albert.

Like · Reply · 2y   👍 3

Penny Fender
Penny #2, I'm still his favorite! 😊
Love you Mr. Albert!

Like · Reply · 2y   👍 2

Sandy Williams
My absolutely favorite teacher ever. Love me some Mr. Albert!!!

Like · Reply · 2y   👍 1

Kelly Steele Johnson
Hello Mr. Albert! A fine man, wonderful teacher! Very patient man, had to point to his mouth and then trash can (get rid of chewing gum) almost every day with me! I thank you and appreciate all you have done for our community! Much love! 😊😊😊

Like · Reply · 2y   👍 2

> **Lynann Mullis**
> Me too. 😊
>
> Like · Reply · 2y

Mollie Lamar
I remember that you **Glenda Ominira Simmons Jenkins** solved a question posed by **Paige Alvarez Hanks** that stumped Mr Albert! Paige wanted to know what caused the brown spots in her family's sugar bowl. He didn't know but you did - It was coffee drops from the spoon used to stir sugar into your parents' coffee. They must have like at least two spoons worth apparently. That always struck me as most clever of you!

Like · Reply · 2y   1

> **Glenda Ominira Simmons Jenkins**
> **Mollie**, what? Oh, my gosh. Between you and **Shawn**, with your super memories, I am truly feeling like an old fogie. **Paige**, do you remember this? Mr. Albert without fail always talks about our class because we would ask him for a few minutes before our lesson to discuss the ERA. I just learned that whem he was in Japan during the Korean War he had to identify human remains. He was really a gift of a teacher.
>
> Like · Reply · 2y · Edited

> **Paige Alvarez Hanks**
> I have absolutely no memory of this but it sure made me smile! Mr. Albert was one of my absolute favorite teachers who inspired me throughout my career as an educator! Miss seeing him and miss you all!
>
> Like · Reply · 2y   2

Corrie Boatwright
Awesome man great teacher

Like · Reply · 2y   1

Linda Morris
Thank you Mr Albert for teaching me some life lessons!

Like · Reply · 2y   2

Tracy Hand Bunch
Great teacher!   4

Like · Reply · 2y

Cindy Hyers Crawford
Great Teacher and I believe everyone respected him.

Like · Reply · 1y   1

Chelsea Adams McFadden
Best teacher EVER!!!

Like · Reply · 2y   2

Michelle Cunningham
Best Teacher & Godly man ever!

Like · Reply · 1y

[51]

Janet Jones
Mr Albert was a great teacher and is a man of honesty and integrity!!!!

Like · Reply · 1y · Edited

Amanda Gail Williams
He was an, amazing, caring man and definitely one of my favorite teachers

Like · Reply · 1y

John Edwards
Mr Albert will always be known for his smile and being a negotiator a brilliant mind

Like · Reply · 1y

Lucy Karrys
What an amazing tribute ! Mayor maybe someone could copy all these comments and make them into a book for. Mr . Albert .

Like · Reply · 1y

Lori Miller
I love Mr. Albert! One of my favorite teachers!

Like · Reply · 1y

Angela Cecil Binney
11. Mr. Albert was an awesome Science teacher at FBJH from when to when (?) not sure. I was in his 8th grade class in 1981!

Like · Reply · 1y   ♡ 1

Karen Rowland Batten
Loved Mr.Albert..great teacher and caring, compassionate man!!!

Like · Reply · 1y   ♡ 1

Melissa Walker
Great throwback!! One of my favorite teachers! I salute you Mr. Albert!!

Like · Reply · 2y

Clint McQuarry
Hey Mr. Albert! Great to see you, Sir!!!

Like · Reply · 1y   ♡ 1

Patricia Russell
Great man inside and out. Thanks for all you have done 🖤

Like · Reply · 1y

Renee Zieglmeier
Mr. Albert was my 8th grade Science teacher I believe.

Like · Reply · 2y

Andrea Witwer
Blessed to have such an amazing man respresenting our community!

Like · Reply · 2y

Will Evans

My little league coach and Middle school Teacher. GREAT MAN !

Like · Reply · 2y

VJames Jones

Yep I gave many memories from Mr. Albert. All of us who attended Peck.

Like · Reply · 2y

Jennifer Keiter

He was a great teacher!!!🖤

Like · Reply · 2y

Felix Boyd Jr.

Yep we had fun coaching against the old man love you mr Albert

Like · Reply · 1y

Gene Aspy

Charles is one of a kind. Great guy.

Like · Reply · 1y

Ryan Stephens

He was my 5th grade teacher one of my favorite

Like · Reply · 1y

Karen Parrish Evans

I love this man! He is the best!!

Like · Reply · 1y

JamaicanJoy Allen

Well done my neighbor...lots of love and blessings continually...

Like · Reply · 2y

James Kevin Drury

He was the one who talked into football in Junior high

Like · Reply · 1y   👍 1

> **James Kevin Drury**
>
> Talked me into football
>
> Like · Reply · 1y

Brian Drawdy

Congrats Mr. Albert. He kept me inline with all those "Longform" threats

Like · Reply · 2y

Carlesa Kirkland-Glover

Like · Reply · 1y

Crystal Peeples Nelson

🖤🖤🖤

Like · Reply · 2y

Christy Drury Youngblood

Awesome teacher 🖤

Like · Reply · 1y

Guy Price

God bless you Mr. Albert

Like · Reply · 1y

Beatrice Alderman

Mr. Albert is the greatest.

Like · Reply · 2y

Sirena Medick

One of my favorite teachers

Like · Reply · 2y

Jeannette Hughley

MR ALBERT WAS THEBESTAND GREATEST TEACHER AT PECK HIGH...HE LOVED HIS STUDENT AND WE LOVED HIM, WE WILL ALWAYS LOVE MR. ALBERT...

Like · Reply · 1y

Kimberly Parker

One of my favorites!!!

Like · Reply · 1y

Beverlt George

Very nice

Like · Reply · 2y

Margo J. Story

Wow!!

Like · Reply · 1y

Julie C Powell
I remember Mr Albert as my teacher also.. Loved him... Great Man...

Like · Reply · 2y   2

Eldolphus Holmes
He was a great coach and teacher to me!!

Like · Reply · 2y   1

Holly Cline
Mr. Albert is such an amazing person. It's an honor to have been one of his students.

Like · Reply · 2y   1

Carla Jones Bates
I smile when i think back to your science class, you made learning fun. Melanie Bird and I had a blast reciting all the bones! Your influence on others is incredible! 🖤

Like · Reply · 2y   2

Lorena Rucker
One of the finest men I've known. I have been honored to call him teacher & friend.

Like · Reply · 2y   1

Rhiannon Joyner
Favorite science teacher!!

Like · Reply · 2y   1

Michelle Davis
It was an honor to have been taught by him. I will always treasure the truly positive example of Leadership and Service he represents to our community!

Like · Reply · 2y · Edited   2

Sandy Mellin
Mr. Albert was a great teacher and is a great man. I teach at the school he taught all of us at!

Like · Reply · 2y   1

Herman Raysor
Proud of you.

Like · Reply · 1y

Gwen Musgrove-Mixon
Linda Jackson

Like · Reply · 2y

Greg Hogan
Ronald Etheridge Jr my favorite teacher and a famu alumni!

Like · Reply · 1y   1

> **Ronald Etheridge Jr**
> **Greg Hogan** Respect there brother nothing but love here 🙏🙏🙏🙏🙏
>
> Like · Reply · 1y · Edited   1

Rachel LeSage
🖤🖤🖤🖤   2
Like · Reply · 2y

[55]

Civic Leadership

Charles Albert served as President of the Nassau County Community Development Corporation (NCCDC), alongside Mrs. Annette Myers, Vice-President. This non-profit chartered organization was founded in 1979, under leadership of the late Elmo Myers, in the interest of saving and restoring now Historic Peck High School. The NCCDC awards scholarships to high school seniors across Nassau County, in addition to projects involving senior citizens.

His awards and community initiatives include:

- American Beach Homeowner's Association
- Board of Directors at Nassau County Volunteer Center
- Chamber of Commerce
- Council on Aging
- Elsie Harper Volunteer of the Year Award
- Governor's Task Force for Reorganization of H.R.S.
- Juvenile Delinquent Council
- NAACP
- Paula Hawkins Commission of Education
- Police Athletic League (PAL)
- President, Nassau County Teacher's Association
- Rotary Club
- Special Olympics
- Take Stock in Children
- Who's Who Among American Educators

Tenure

Mayoral duties play a critical role in local government. Those duties consist of but are not limited to, long meeting after meeting while acclimating to the business, private, and public sectors. The expectations are high: a balanced, relatable, and people-oriented personality, a leader who will speak up on behalf of his or her constituents, and actively consider the citizens and the city's needs. If a mayoral candidate appears to lack these qualities, there is usually little hope of being elected or re-elected. The ability to drive change, alongside a supportive, knowledgeable team, and maintain that momentum throughout the term requires considerable executive acumen.

***

Charles L. Albert Jr.

I enjoyed community initiatives. If there were a choice between sitting around doing nothing or taking some action, I would choose the latter. No doubt, there were numerous opportunities for change and improvement within the City of Fernandina. A child's parent (Mr. Louis Williams) recognized my potential while I was coaching Little League. He followed me home one day, and we talked privately in the garage.

Louis said, "Albert, there's something I want to discuss with you, and I want you to give it serious thought."

He suggested I would be a good fit for city commissioner. Yes, I initially hesitated; it was a colossal task to undertake. Although it has always been a dream of mine, politics was not on my radar at that time. I was wrestling with his suggestion that I run for office. When I was a kid, my dad warned me to stay away from politics and never be a policeman. But my mama told me, "...one day you will see a Black man become President," and on January 20, 2009, I was encouraged and excited to witness what mama foretold.

Several friends and people from all races in the community unified, encouraged, and kept after me. A few of them even insinuated I was crazy to run for mayor against such a powerful sitting candidate. I consistently refused to run, but they were relentless. My wife and I discussed it in detail. I saw an opportunity to make a difference, and then I proudly accepted the challenge.

It's finally Election Day, and the votes are being counted— we had no technology. While all the candidates were standing around waiting on the results, one of them approached me and made a statement that shook my confidence a bit.

"Mr. Albert, I want you to know; if you don't win, do not give up, try again." I started thinking, "...Oh my Lord, what does this person know?" Sure enough, the results came back, and the people shouted, "Albert Won!"

A journalist in the crowd questioned the conceding candidate. "You didn't win this time; how do you feel?"

I remember part of the reply was, "I feel like the dickens!"

Conceding a defeat can be a bitter pill to swallow, but ultimately the transfer of power was honorable, orderly, and peaceful. Every day wasn't easy, but I have absolutely no regrets about serving the City of Fernandina.

***

1978 – 1980	City Commissioner, Fernandina Beach, FL
1980 – 1981	Vice-Mayor
1981 – 1982	Mayor of Fernandina Beach, FL
1984 – 1986	Vice-Mayor
1986 – 1987	Mayor of Fernandina Beach, FL
1989 – 1990	Vice-Mayor
1991 – 1992	Vice-Mayor
1993	Declined Mayoral Nomination
1994 – 1996	Mayor of Fernandina Beach, FL

Developing Town

Fernandina Beach has a rich cultural history of Black Americans who served the town in an official capacity as justice of the peace, county commissioner, mayor, deputy sheriff, tax accessor, and treasurer.

Disembarked and no longer legally slaves, the Delaney family of twelve settled in Fernandina in 1865 at the end of the Civil War. The patriarch, A.M.E. Pastor, and skilled ship carpenter Thomas Delaney served as Nassau County Voter Registrar within two years of his family's arrival via rowboat. Possibly following his lead, more than thirty Black men aggressively sought positions in governmental politics and served on the city council through the year 1902.

In 1981, seventy-nine years later, Fernandina Beach elected its first Black mayor since the end of the Civil War and the Reconstruction Era purporting social equality for Black men and women (1865-1877). Community advocate Charles L. Albert Jr. had work to do on Amelia Island. As the town continued to develop, its forecasted socio-economic demographics increased at a rate of approximately 20-percent during his tenure (Fernandina Beach Census 1960-2010).

Albert stands for unity and equality with every fiber of his being. By doing so, sometimes uncomfortably, he has contributed to the improvement and forward movement of race relations in Fernandina Beach during and after his tenure. Patricia Thompson, the first Black female city commissioner and vice-mayor (2001-2002), and others, have all successfully walked through doors opened, to some extent, because Charles L. Albert Jr. unselfishly answered the call to civic leadership.

Forever Friendships

The young Aaron Bean played Little League on the segregated team, and when it wasn't popular, Charles L. Albert Jr. was breaking through racial barriers to integrate Little League for Black kids. Their paths crossed in middle school. Soon the student/teacher relationship morphed into a friendship that forever changed the course of Aaron Bean's life. Like many of Mr. Albert's former students have attested, he too was inspired to excel.

Senator Aaron Bean:

He was one of the absolute very best 8th-grade science teachers at Fernandina Beach Middle School (1981-1992). I remember him fondly; gifted, able to hold your attention, always writing formulas, and performing captivating experiments. If I could not have fainted at the sight of blood, I could have gone on to be a doctor! That's how well he taught science.

Then, there is his political side. Our hometown resembled Mayberry's fictional town from the 1960s sitcom, *The Andy Griffith Show*; everybody knew each other. I watched as Mr. Albert transitioned from an educator to the mayor. We were always cognizant of the threat of "big development" destroying the island's character and essence. Charles L. Albert Jr. was instrumental in its aesthetic preservation and race relations within our community.

In the 1980s, my dad served with him on the Fernandina Beach City Council. Years later, I followed my dad's footsteps and won a seat on the city commission. I subsequently followed Mr. Albert's lead and was elected mayor.

The leap of courage where I will forever be in Mr. Albert's debt was in the year 2000. I campaigned for Congressman in the House of Representatives (Florida). I was not expected to win because Democrats outnumbered Republicans two-to-one. My consultant asked me if I had any Democratic friends who would endorse me. My friend, Charles Albert, said, "Bean, I will be with you." I know Mr. Albert took some heat for that; he took some blowback, but he stuck with me, and I'm forever grateful to him.

Interestingly, I was one of the last students to attend now Historic Peck High School, just before it closed. I was in the third grade at segregated Southside School (1976). Extensive renovations on our wing caused limited class space. All the third-graders were relocated to Peck High School for half the year, taking up six of their classrooms. When the Fernandina

Beach City Commission received the grant to preserve Peck High and make it home for city and community-based offices, I proudly participated in that ribbon cutting. That's my "claim to fame" memory for a White kid during segregation attending a Black school on that historic landmark in Fernandina Beach.

On a more serious note, in our city, male teachers are a minority; when you incorporate Black teachers, the pool shrinks further. The unicorn in this situation concerns grades "K through Eighth." Black males look up and don't see any teachers that look like them. For this reason, Nassau County has launched a "Race Equality Coalition." Its purpose is to ensure that everyone gets a fair shot. Our goal is to attract creative and skilled Black male teachers like Charles L. Albert Jr. was to me. His community work in Fernandina Beach, Florida, is legendary.

Letter From The Senator

FLORIDA HOUSE OF REPRESENTATIVES
Representative Aaron Bean
District 12

Economic Development, Trade & Banking
Fiscal Council
Future of Florida's Families, Vice Chair

Health Care Appropriations, Chair
Health & Families Council

December 8, 2005

Mr. Charles L. Albert Jr.
██████████████
Fernandina Beach, FL 32034

Dear Mr. Albert:

In my memory, you will always be the Mayor of Fernandina Beach. Your continuous involvement in the community, as a school teacher, coach, City Commissioner, family man and civic leader, truly makes you a man for all seasons.

You have taught biology and chemistry in Nassau County Schools for some 40 years. The most important subject you passed on to your students was leadership, as a coach and then President of Little League. Whenever there was a need for a civic leader, you stepped forward.

In 1978, you made history by being elected as the first black Fernandina Beach City Commissioner since Reconstruction. And what a fine Commissioner you have been, holding the seat some 18 years and being elected as Mayor in 1994 and some 3 other terms as Mayor since then.

Charles and Ernie Albert, you have both given so much to Fernandina Beach, Amelia Island and Nassau County. Your decades of service make me proud to have been a student in your classroom, a Little League player and a former Mayor of Fernandina Beach, I respect your accomplishments. Thank you both so much.

Sincerely,

Aaron Bean
State Representative, District 12

Looking forward to having you and Ernie in Tally this year

Letter From The Governor

STATE OF FLORIDA
OFFICE OF GOVERNOR BOB GRAHAM

August 17, 1982

Honorable Charles L. Albert, Jr.
Mayor
▓▓▓▓▓▓▓▓▓▓
Fernandina Beach, Florida 32034

Dear Mayor Albert:

While I was in Fernandina Beach for a brief vacation last month, I met a student, Kim Cardinelli, who was very complimentary of you and the schools in your area. As the father of four teenage daughters, I know that compliments from them are special treasures and thought you would like to know the positive impression that you have made on this young person.

I also hear good things about the leadership that you are providing to the City of Fernandina Beach, and I was extremely impressed with the city, especially the sensitive historical restoration. If I can be of any assistance to you or the city, I would be pleased to do so.

With kind regards,

Sincerely,

Governor

BG/ce

Race Relations

He was retired from the Nassau County School system and no longer campaigning for mayor, but Charles Albert's mind was never idle. He was always passionate about eradicating racial inequality through education and positive actions. Mr. Albert recounted an article he wrote for the local newspaper during Black History Month.

The initial article, in its entirety, was intended to encourage amicable relationships and cultural diversity. Multiple points of view are recapped via excerpts:

Charles L. Albert Jr.

I'm always intrigued with February, when Black History Month is celebrated. Why focus on just one day? We should realize the importance of this cultural calendar event throughout the year. We've suffered significant losses due to racism, fueled by three main ingredients: money, lack of education, and cultural diversity. Blacks have been called the "N" word and categorized by class based on the melanin in our skin, to shame and control. Reject every negative undertone and focus on the positive actions required to move us forward in society. When our thoughts are apathetic concerning the effects of racial inequality on society, we will miss out on opportunities for personal growth, community growth, and unity. Let's strive to become intelligent thinkers of inventions and time-saving devices to enhance our lives. If our focus is distracted by handouts, then expecting them will ultimately be our way of life. Let's wise up. God did not create an inferior race of humans.

Sunshine State

Mrs. Ernie Tyson-Albert:

"Mrs. Gray, did Charles tell you he was in a movie?"

***

The Honorable Charles L. Albert Jr. made a cameo appearance in the movie *Sunshine State*. Short synopsis: A company wants to buy up everything and turn the location into a high-rise beach resort community. Together with an ensemble cast of 29, including (in alphabetical order) Mary Alice, Angela Bassett, Bill Cobbs, Edie Falco, Miguel Ferrer, Timothy Hutton, James McDaniel, Dennis Neal, Ralph Waite, Charlayne Woodard, and Tom Wright; Mr. Albert played the role of "Reverend Sutcliff."

***

As the movie gig goes, Mr. Albert was riding around, checking on his neighborhood as usual. Mrs. Albert amusingly describes his routine as "...being nosey." If there was an official casting call or audition notice posted, apparently Charles Albert missed it. He wasn't trying to break into the film industry when he drove by the Martin Luther King Jr. Recreation Center one morning to find the parking lot full and a crowd of people inside. Albert, the inquisitive community advocate, went inside and asked questions. He did not identify himself as a former mayor, city commissioner, educator, or Little League coach. A member of the casting team explained that people were auditioning for the role of "preacher" in a movie, and then the woman invited him to stay. Mr. Albert sat down to gain more information. He had no intentions of participating, but the casting team handed him a script on the spot.

Actual ordained preachers were auditioning, along with local actors from surrounding cities. Mr. Albert had a chance to memorize the script of less-than-five lines while watching the others get called onto the stage to read for the casting team privately.

The following day, a casting spokeswoman came to Mr. Albert's home and congratulated him on being selected to play the role of "Reverend Sutcliff." He wondered how he got chosen over the ordained preachers and professional acting hopefuls. Perhaps they over-acted the role while reading their lines. Maybe Charles Albert's unassuming, always calm, professional, and courteous demeanor was what the casting team was looking for as he walked through the doors. The team never revealed the exact reason for their decision.

He never hired an agent; never took acting lessons; he did not show up with a professional photo headshot or a resume`. Unknowingly, Charles L. Albert Jr. snagged a "bit part" that granted him direct interaction with a star-studded cast in a "Sony Pictures Classic," written and directed by John Sayles—even if his appearance was only for a few minutes.

***

Mr. Albert never intentionally looks for the spotlight, it finds him, and then he shines.

Epilogue

She's generally soft-spoken, but today Mrs. Albert's tone is animated and excitedly modulated.

"Oh my, you will not believe what I just found! I was looking for some pictures, and I was digging around in a box. I found this tablet. I'm telling you; you won't believe what's in this tablet!"

I pressed my cellular telephone closer to my ear as if that would reduce the suspense.

"What! Mrs. Albert, tell me, what's in this tablet?"

Mr. Albert had been nurturing another dream by faith. He started freewriting his memoir years ago but never finished. Short stories about his upbringing, concepts, ideas, and conversations he had with himself, are documented in pencil and pen. His undated handwritten thoughts were brainstormed across the page, connected by circles, lines, and arrows.

While pulling together the in-person interviews and notes for his memoir, a battle was happening between my ears. One voice was always encouraging; a gloomy voice repeatedly whispered in my other ear, "...Just keep quiet. It's common knowledge that Black Americans have managed to accomplish great things." What's common is that history books had little to say about the positive contributions of Black Americans and their peaceful affiliations with people whose demographics or political views may have been quite different. When we survey Black History from state-to-state, the Alberts' story may not be unique, but it certainly should not be left untold.

There is a grace and favor on Mr. Albert's life that, to this day, causes people to use their power, influence, and ability to help him. The capacity to perform whenever there is a need, without official training, is how he could introduce Little League Baseball to Black youth during segregation, even though it was suggested they could not learn the rules or play the sport. When he dreamed of becoming mayor, he never imagined a baseball field in his hometown would someday bear his name. In the 1950s, his sincere desire to be a peacemaker and community advocate facilitated an amicable relationship with law enforcement. That relationship often prevented Black males from frivolously going to jail or worse.

Without asking him the details, I'm confident there were adverse situations to endure, uncomfortable conversations to mediate, things he could not share with me, and undoubtedly, people whose presence initially disturbed him. In the notes he penned, Mr. Albert reflected on two words coined as his "two steps of life," common sense. Combining wisdom with common sense always revealed the appropriate way to reciprocate, relate, and resolve any situation he faced.

***

In December of 2020, his health rapidly declined. Home Hospice facilitated medical care; his family ensured he remained comfortable, secure, and in good spirits.

Early in life, this humble man of faith recognized how wise choices, education, and using his voice to make a difference could cause a city to flourish. It didn't seem impossible to him—that he would facilitate change and help his community thrive. It wasn't a ridiculous thought that a Black chemistry, math, biology, and science teacher would positively impact and mentor students across racial divides. I am beyond grateful for the opportunity to have personally interviewed this gentle giant. Each living generation would do well to remember three things from Charles Albert's journey:

1. Dreams do come true if while you're waiting, you're also becoming an asset and not a liability.
2. The word "impossible" cannot co-exist with your dreams.
3. The journey ahead of you will be challenging, but as The Honorable Charles L. Albert Jr. has proven, challenges are designed to be conquered.

Lest We Forget

The Honorable Ed Boner

"I remember Charles Albert for the impression he left. He never sought the spotlight. At first glance, I saw someone unassuming, humble, and someone willing to listen. He always impressed me as genuinely caring about your views. It isn't surprising he became a fixture on the commission. It speaks volumes to see accomplishments like the Elm Street Little League, political leadership, and church leadership. He was a leader because he was willing to work selflessly and because he cared about everyone—and that's something we truly need in every generation."

The Honorable Arlene Filkoff

"When you have things named after you, folks know you're special—you could feel it in his presence. Charles Albert contributed his 'do the right thing' values, generosity of spirit, and his wisdom: '...you might not always win, but you always learn something'."

The Honorable Joe Gerrity

"Charles Albert was in his final term when I arrived in Fernandina Beach in 1994. Many spoke of him with great respect. As commissioner and mayor, I came to know him through the Elm Street Little League, which he founded. I remember the pride he displayed in the coaches and the team players. He always included everyone, and I still have a baseball he signed for me."

The Honorable Bruce Malcolm

"I knew former mayor Albert by reputation. His was one of the first names I heard when we moved to Fernandina Beach in 1988. When passing me on the street, he would always nod in recognition. He knew who I was, and that made me proud; a grand legacy for a grand gentleman."

The Honorable Kim Page

"He is a trailblazer and visionary. Charles Albert served as mayor, but his real gift to our community was his ability to inspire generations of local students to be the best version of themselves. His gifts are immeasurable."

The Honorable Ron Sapp

"I served five terms (15 years) with my fellow mayor. He was big news—the first African American to be elected, a gentleman, great listener, a local statesman, a responsive representative, never comfortable with contention among commissioners. Fernandina is a better place because of him."

The Honorable Susan H. Steger

"In an era of intense racial strife, Charles Albert moved our city forward with gentle kindness and respect. We will remember his impact on our community for generations to come."

Memories

Mrs. Ernie Tyson-Albert:
Our 60th Wedding Anniversary; the band was playing inside the Elm Street Recreation Center. Charles was happy and content to stay at his table and enjoy everything, but his daughter and former students pulled him onto the dance floor. The band played one of his favorite songs, "Mustang Sally."

BOTH PHOTOS COURTESY OF GLENDA JENKINS-SIMMONS

Charles Albert stops to chat with Wendall K. McGahee during his first (2020) campaign for city commissioner.

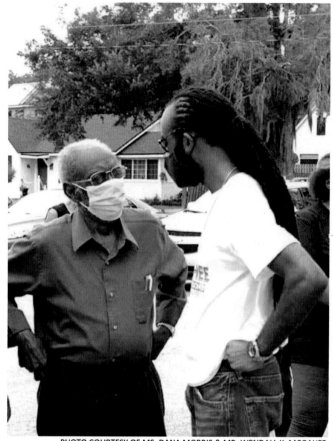

PHOTO COURTESY OF MS. DANA MORRIS & MR. WENDALL K. MCGAHEE

Charles L. Albert, Jr. being sworn into office
as City Commissioner - Fernandina Beach, Florida

PHOTO COURTESY OF CHARLES & ERNIE ALBERT

March 1996 - Downtown Fernandina Beach
Mayor Albert headed to Shriner's parade.

Mrs. Ernie Tyson Albert Library, Ceremony October 2019
(Library Marker Resolution #2019-89)

IMAGE COURTESY CITY OF FERNANDINA BEACH FACEBOOK PAGE

The Elsie Harper Volunteer Award (2001)

Celebrating with the apple of his eye, Ernie Tyson-Albert

[81]

The Honorable Charles L. Albert Jr. representing his
alma mater (now Historic Peck High) on his jacket.

A man of faith, Bro. Charles L. Albert, Steward Pro-Tem,
Prince Chapel A.M.E. Church, 60+ years

Proclamation

WHEREAS, active participation by youth in appropriate physical activities contributes to their fitness and to the enhancement of our community's quality of life; and

WHEREAS, the Little League baseball organization was started in 1939 and not only promotes the physical well-being of the players, but also instills into them the qualities of fairness, cooperation, and discipline-qualities which contribute to the development of good citizenship; and

WHEREAS, in 1974 the Little League revised its rules to support participation by girls by creating a Girls' Softball program; and

WHEREAS, Little Leagues in communities throughout our Nation have made it possible for thousands of young boys and girls to take an active part in our national game of baseball; and

WHEREAS, the Elm Street Little League was formed in our community in 1967 under the guidance of Mr. Charles Albert Jr., Mr. Esdene Handsome and Deputy Curtis Telfair to promote the ideals of the Little League organization and is open to all eligible youth regardless of their financial capabilities; and

WHEREAS, Mr. Albert and Elm Street League officials have constantly stressed that education is the key to any and all success in life for the youth; and

WHEREAS, a Girls' Softball program was introduced under the Elm Street Little League's Charter in 2012 and they will be practicing and playing their games at Joe Velardi field; and

WHEREAS, the players, coaches, parents and other friends of the Elm Street Little League have volunteered thousands of hours of their time to support the operation of the Elm Street Little League.

NOW, THEREFORE, I, Arlene R. Filkoff, by virtue of the authority vested in me as Mayor of the City of Fernandina Beach, Florida, do hereby designate the second (2nd) week of June, 2012, as:

"ELM STREET LITTLE LEAGUE BASEBALL WEEK"

in Fernandina Beach, Florida and I invite the people of Fernandina Beach to observe that week in parks, athletic fields, and other suitable places with appropriate activities designed to emphasize the importance of the physical development of our youth.

IN WITNESS WEREOF, I hereunto set my hand and cause the Official Seal of the City of Fernandina Beach, Florida to be affixed this 5th day of June 2012.

CITY OF FERNANDINA BEACH

Arlene R. Filkoff
Commissioner - Mayor

IMAGE COURTESY OF CHARLES & ERNIE ALBERT

Charles L. Albert Jr. Field
Elm Street Little League
(MLK Jr. Park)

Thank you for your service!

Charles Laverne Albert Jr.

Sunrise:
Wednesday June 29, 1932

Sunset:
Sunday, January 24, 2021

Acknowledgments

Mr. and Mrs. Charles L. Albert Jr., and Family
You granted me in-person recorded interviews and access to your personal archives. Thank you for trusting me with Charles Albert's dream.

State Senator Aaron Bean
The Florida Senate, 4th District
Thank you for the candid interview and your narrative in support of Charles Albert's memoir.

Fernandina Beach Mayor Elect,
The Honorables, and the Nassau County Sheriff
Thank you for sharing your comments honoring his legacy.

Collection of Comments
Facilitated by Caroline Best, CMC, City Clerk
City of Fernandina Beach Government

Drs. James and Terresa White, the author's Pastors:
In great appreciation for the encouragement, God-inspired principles, and affirmations that you've instilled

Saul S. Goffin's letter to the U.S. Postal Service
Amelia Island Museum of History, Fernandina Beach, Florida
Electronic archived images and excerpts

The Delaney Family
Article Excerpt, by Kevin Turner, The Florida Times-Union, "Blacks Once Controlled Fernandina Politics; between 1869 and 1902, 42 African-American Men Held Local Elective Office." Originally retrieved: 08/18/2020, Questia.com.

Developing Town
Fernandina Beach Census 1960-2010

Made in the USA
Middletown, DE
17 February 2023

25107438R00053